ENCOUNTERS with the
LIVING JESUS

*Personal Stories from
an Ordinary Mystic*

ENCOUNTERS
with the
LIVING JESUS

Personal Stories from an
Ordinary Mystic

❋

Diane G. H. Kilmer

Encounters with the Living Jesus:
Personal Stories from an Ordinary Mystic

J M Press, Inc.
Printed in the United States of America
Copyright © 2009 by Diane G. H. Kilmer

ISBN 978-0-578-04254-1

Scripture quotations, unless otherwise noted, are from the Holy Bible, New Revised Standard Version (NRSV), copyright © 1989, Division of Christian Education of the National Council of the Churches of Christ in the United States of America. Used by permission. All rights reserved.

Book design by Christina Nelson, at http://www.sunlitnook.com
Full cover design copyright © 2009 by Christina Nelson
"Sparkly" brushes used throughout from http://www.obsidiandawn.com/ Used by permission.
Pottery, beadwork art & photos for cover and interior copyright © *Yatsar*. Used by permission.
Photograph of the author copyright © Jane D. Kilmer at www.flickr.com/photos/kilmerphotography

This book is dedicated to my parents,
Gene and Wanda Hatcher,
who started me on my spiritual path,
and to my children,
David and Jane Kilmer,
who live lives of faith that are
applicable to their time and culture.

CONTENTS

MADE-UP TRUE STORIES

COMMUNION MEDITATIONS

Introduction

During prayer, when I asked Jesus if He had any suggestions about how I could celebrate my 60th birthday (March 3, 2009), one idea that immediately came to mind was to write down and publish some of my stories. These particular stories describe key moments in my life when I am absolutely certain God came near. Core faith experiences such as these continue to influence how I live my life. Even when I recall them now, years later, they evoke tears and wonder and faith.

In this collection are also two fictional stories born out of need and prayer, plus a few communion meditations gleaned from my prayer journals.

My hope is that the Spirit will use these writings to encourage others to seek deeper intimacy with Jesus all of their lives.

All Glory to God,

Diane G. H. Kilmer
September 2009

Encounters

What If It's Really True?

YOU COULD SAY I'd been a pretty good Christian girl up to now — "now" being my senior year in high school.

I loved God, and I tried to do everything that I knew of to please God. The church I grew up in taught me that it would please God if I: didn't dance; didn't smoke; didn't drink alcohol; didn't show too much emotion in worship; didn't expect to lead in prayer, or singing, or teaching or preaching; didn't expect crosses or other sacred art in God's house; didn't expect the Holy Spirit to move in any other way except through the Bible.

So I didn't.

I also didn't date guys outside of my church. Didn't apply to colleges not affiliated with my church. Didn't expect much for myself nor my future. Didn't. Didn't. Didn't.

One spring day during that last year of high school, I was feeling kind of empty and restless about all the didn'ts in my religion. And I thought to myself: *Is that all there is?*

I didn't pray it. I just thought it, once.

The following Sunday I meandered into the church's library, which consisted of one bookshelf attached to the wall, just above a crib in the nursery. As my eyes swept over those books, one title jumped out at me: *Your God Is Too Small*, written by J.B. Phillips.[1] The title was so audacious, so insulting, that I just had to have a look at it. So

I picked it up and took it home.

At my house, trying to be alone with a book was nearly impossible. My three younger sisters and I shared one big attic bedroom; there was very little privacy.

So the next day, in order to read this book in peace and quiet, I told my mom I wasn't feeling well and needed to stay home from school. She called the school before she and dad left for work. Once everybody was out of the house, I settled down on the candy-striped carpet of my bedroom floor and started reading *Your God Is Too Small*.

The book was divided into two parts. The first half described all these images of God that were too small and too limiting, such as "Resident Policeman," "God in a Box," "Grand Old Man in the Sky," "Pale Galilean," etc.

The second half of the book talked about Jesus in such a fresh, new way to me, that it completely shifted my thinking.

The author talked about how God was really too big, too great, too incomprehensible for us created humans to understand. In fact, people's understanding of who God is had gotten into such a confused state, (which God knew would happen), that God made a plan to come In Person to clear up all the misunderstandings about who God is. God wanted to show us how to live the kind of fulfilling life God had created human beings to live in the first place.

The problem was (and I'm putting this into my own words), if God came in all of God's Hugeness and Power and Intelligence and Spectacular-ness, we humans would probably melt, or something. And even if we lived after the encounter, we'd be too frightened to become friends with such a Visitor.

And God wanted to be friends.

To solve this problem, the author explained, God planned to "focus" God's entire self—everything that is "true" and "real" about God—into a small, focused window that humans *could* comprehend. When people looked through this window to God, — a window that actually *was* God — people would be able to know who God is and what God is *really* like.

No more guessing or too-small-of-views, I thought to myself. People would be able to walk right up next to God and get a closer look and become friends, God hoped.

So God limited God's very Self, and condensed all of God's god-qualities into a tiny, non-threatening, approachable form. As Phillips put it: God visited Planet Earth as "Human Baby A."

Suddenly, all the stories I'd ever heard in Sunday school came back to me, supporting this idea of "God focused" into a human package.

I thought of the Hebrew nation anticipating a coming Messiah.

I thought of the fresh womb of a young Jewish girl, through whom God made entry into God's own universe.

I thought about the vulnerable circumstances in which God placed God's very Self — circumstances that led all the way to death.

And God did all this just to communicate with us creatures.

God did all this just to invite us into relationship with our own Creator.

God did all this to be known and to know how life is for us people living down here in our messiness, alongside hints of grandeur.

God came to clear up a few questions and to teach us a better way to live.

God came to show God's friends that there is Life after death.

God came to save us.

And I thought to myself, *What if it's really true? What if Jesus really is the Son of God?!?!?!*

And suddenly I knew — deep down to my core — that it was true! I believed that Jesus really is the Son of God!

I felt like I'd discovered new news! I had believed the gospel before, but this felt different! My understanding felt broader, deeper. The truth seemed fresh. Astonishing. And I felt joyous! Buoyant! Glad that Jesus had come!

Then suddenly, right after all this reasoning and acceptance and joy, Jesus came into my room.

I'm not kidding. He actually showed up. In front of me; a little to my right. Standing. With the outline of His body and face glowing with a light so bright I couldn't bear to look at it.

So I went flat on my face on the carpet, nose buried into the candy-stripe carpet, arms stretched above my head toward the Figure, thinking on the way down, *So this is why people go prostrate!*

But I could still see Him in my mind, pouring this Light and Love toward me and into me. The Love just kept radiating over me, intensely, going on and on for I don't know how long until I finally thought, *I don't know how long I can bear this much love.*

As soon as I thought that thought, Jesus gently... kindly...receded from the room.

But His image was burned on my brain, like a brand, still there more than 40 years later.

Jesus answered my question "Is that all there is?" by leading me to a book that led my mind and heart and soul to Him. By showing up in my bedroom that day, Jesus revealed to me: "I Am the Something More you are looking for. I love you. I Am alive. And if I Am alive, anything is possible!"

My God is not too small.

The Still Center of the Storm

IT WAS A dark and stormy night. We were newlyweds, my spouse and I, driving in the middle of the night "straight through" to Abilene, Texas, from Michigan after our honeymoon. All our worldly possessions were packed behind us in a small U-haul trailer attached to the used car my new in-laws had given us as a wedding present.

Now I strained to see the road ahead through a watery, blurred windshield, while my husband slept soundly in the passenger seat next to me. The dashboard clock said 3 a.m. The adrenaline rush that had come with the exhilaration of being on our own, headed to our first home, had all drained away. My eyelids were becoming too heavy to keep open—I needed to pull over and sleep.

But there had been no sign of civilization for hours; no parking lot or rest stop or any break in the relentlessly narrow, bare, no-shoulder, two-lane highway. Finally, my rain-dulled headlights revealed a wide shoulder of road just ahead, a slight rise with overgrown bushes that offered safety from this torrential flooding. In the blinding rain, I parked on the rise, turned off the engine, and expected to fall right to sleep. But instead, in the darkness, I felt an urgent nagging inside me to back the car off of the rise—trailer and all.

Without thinking, I obeyed the urge, too exhausted

to argue with such irrationality. I turned the key, reversed the gear, and rolled straight back a foot or two. Since I don't remember a thing after that, I probably fell asleep within seconds of shutting off the engine.

I don't know how long I'd been asleep, when suddenly a loud, thunderous BOOM! startled us awake. The continuous roar rolling only inches in front of our car materialized in the downpour into a passing train speeding along its track. I quickly realized that my first parking spot had been directly on a railroad track! My obedience to the urgent feeling had saved us.

I didn't know it right then, but eventually, over time, I came to believe that those pressing, restless urges are one of the ways the Holy Spirit of Jesus communicates with me, sometimes even warning me of danger. Of course, I can't prove it and a few other possible explanations can be suggested — all equally unprovable.

But over the past four decades these nudges sometimes come from a Voice I can recognize who tells me the truth, comforts me, gives me direction, and reminds me of what I've already learned so that I can stay on the road toward spiritual safety and maturity. This unseen Helper behaves exactly as Jesus had promised to His worried disciples the night before He died. So I pay attention.

What Do I Really Need?

THERE I WAS again, kneeling down next to my bed in Japan, crying and begging God for the gift of tongues. He had turned me down twice and this was my third time to ask.

I was 23, married for two years, and terribly home-sick. As missionary teachers my husband and I had signed two-year contracts to teach English during the day; we taught Bible classes in our home at night. At first being a missionary in the Far East had seemed like a glamorous adventure. But the glamour wore off very quickly. I soon discovered that "seed planting" work—as missionaries liked to call it—was usually not that exciting. I missed my family, but it cost too much to fly home for a visit, and long-distance phone calls in those days weren't really an affordable option.

Adding to my sense of isolation were the letters from family and friends back home in the United States that described the huge wave of charismatic gifts of the Holy Spirit that were sweeping through most of the American churches and around the world. It was the early 1970s, and the exciting news of many people I knew being able to pray in strange languages made me long to experience this gift and anything else God might be doling out. I didn't want to feel farther from home and happenings than I already felt.

So here I was on my knees again, pleading

for this gift, when suddenly I heard a loud voice say, *No! Now don't ask Me again. Get up and wipe your tears.* I immediately jumped up to a standing position and started wiping my face before I even knew what I was doing. The Voice continued, *I have given you the gift of faith, and that is enough for now.*

Surprised by the Voice and its clear instruction, I walked out of my bedroom and decided to stop wishing that I were someplace else. From then on, I tried harder to be content where I had been planted.

This incident early in my life marked the beginning experience of several prayer lessons for me: to seek the Giver more than the gift; to ask Jesus "What do I need?" more often than telling Him what I need; and to trust that Jesus will give me the spiritual graces I really need at just the right time. On this occasion at my bedside forty years ago, Jesus spoke directly into my mind in my own native tongue for the very first time. To that lonely young woman living in another culture so far from home, He gave the perfect gift.

Sometimes I think that Jesus might surprise me someday with a new prayer language for some special occasion. But I will never ask!

Getting Into Hot Water

I DREADED STRIPPING down in front of villagers and being boiled like a lobster.

Since the moment our missionary team had agreed to help out with a gospel meeting in a southern coastal city on Honshu Island, Japan, I had worried obsessively. The meeting would be held during the hottest part of the summer, and I would have to use a neighborhood public bathhouse while we were there.

I was only 23 — a modest, compliant, newly-wedded young woman from Michigan who, in the early 1970s, had been recruited right out of college alongside my young husband to teach English in Japan. During the day, we taught at a four-school campus; at night we held Bible studies in our home, which was also on campus. Our Western-style house provided — among other cultural luxuries — bathroom privacy, which had given me a level of comfort in an otherwise unfamiliar culture.

A sick feeling pervaded the pit of my stomach about using a public bath, even after all the praying. My first concern was having to undress in front of all the town women who would also be using the *ofuro*, their word for "bath." My fair skin, blonde hair and European features had drawn attention in Japan from day one. Everywhere I went, people stared. At first I enjoyed this movie star treatment.

But by the end of six months, I longed for an anonymity that was not possible in a country where I stood out like a white dot on a black domino. I had no doubt that when I bathed at the *ofuro*, everyone would stare.

But the second issue was pure fear of the hot bath water. My calves were nearly scalded once at a quaint little inn in Nara. Another time when I was a guest in a Japanese home, my hosts graciously gave me "first dip" rights, before everyone else in the family took turns using the same water for soaking. They poured my bath water in a kind of barrel-shaped tub, and then left the room. I tried, but I couldn't sit longer than a minute in that *ofuro* before I felt like screaming. It wasn't just me having a low tolerance for hot water. Japanese newspaper articles were reporting that the commonly extreme *ofuro* temperatures were lowering men's sperm counts!

Imagining myself at the upcoming public bath, I pictured a crowd of native women watching me step down into the large in-ground bath, observing the *gaijin* — the foreigner — writhing in agony while they comfortably tolerated the heat, and then laughing as I quickly climbed out, my skin clean — but covered in second-degree burns. I couldn't wait.

Three days into the mission week, I couldn't put off bathing any longer. Two upper-income, Japanese college girls who had accompanied our team had also never bathed in public. Together, we dragged our feet to the bathhouse, paid our money, and followed the hallway fork to the left toward the women's side of the facility. Soon wrapped modestly in towels, our clothes stuffed into lockers, we carefully entered what I call the pre-wash room like deer stepping into an open meadow. Around the large, fully-tiled room, spigots had been installed about knee-high. Small stools and little buckets sat near each faucet so that bathers could wash themselves completely before heading outdoors to soak in the 12 x 9 foot bath.

I washed and washed and washed myself, waiting for those two girls to lead the way to the *ofuro* and thus serve as distractions from my own entrance. But they were dawdling the same way I was. I wonder why I didn't just dry off, get dressed and leave; I was certainly clean. But at that time, for whatever reason, I felt compelled to complete the entire, proper bathing ritual.

Finally, I couldn't postpone the dreaded bath any longer. For days I had prayed that Jesus would deliver me from certain public humiliation; so far, He hadn't. I needed to get it over with, so I told the girls I was going in.

Swiftly I walked outdoors over to the steps leading down into a bathing container that resembled a room-sized baptismal tank to me. Instead of a crowd, only two or three ancient Japanese women were there, soaking in water up to their necks. Their facial skin appeared dark and leathery and deeply lined, probably from working long days in the rice fields; *skin toughened enough to protect them from the hot water,* I thought to myself. I took a big breath, let the towel drop and quickly descended the steps, immersing up to my chin.

To my astonishment, the water temperature felt tepid! Moderately warm! Lukewarm, even. And very, very comfortable to my skin, like Michigan lake water in August. I exhaled the tension that had accumulated for weeks. My muscles relaxed as my body floated a little and I playfully moved my arms around a few strokes, though this was probably not proper *ofuro* etiquette. All I could think of was that a whole village was not staring at me and the bath water was not burning my skin. All that worry for nothing.

My peaceful thoughts were suddenly interrupted by screams coming from behind me. I turned around to see my two companions now in the water near the steps, faces in agony, bodies bobbing up and down in what apparently, to them, felt like hot, boiling water. The two young women remained in the bath about 15 seconds, then escaped, rushing back inside.

My mind took a long moment to sort through its confusion before I could acknowledge what had happened: God, I believed, had done something out of the ordinary for me.

I don't know how He did it any more than Shadrach, Meshach, and Abednego knew how they didn't burn up in the fire or their clothes not even smelling like smoke. But those Old Testament characters were taking a public stand for God. Why would God go out of His way supernaturally for a fearful young woman who simply wanted to avoid personal embarrassment? And are deliverances always done in unexpected ways? Must we always enter the fire (or hot water) first?

Letting go of my questions, I began to focus my eyes on the peaceful garden that surrounded the bath like the setting for a jewel. I eased the back of my neck down onto the tiled, curved edge of the *ofuro*, allowing my near-weightless limbs to rest, suspended in the liquid mercy.

My Jewish Sister

IT WAS UNUSUAL for me to be in the same room anymore when the TV news was on. Early in my marriage I had stopped watching television news broadcasts. Those 60-second clips of bad news and violence felt like assaults on my empathetic heart, so I kept up with the world by reading my news, instead.

But on that one evening in 1978, I got caught off guard. I was peacefully settled on the couch, nursing my brand new baby son, when my husband – a television news junkie back then – came home from work and turned on the evening news.

The news broadcaster was introducing a report describing a random attack on a Jewish family by Palestinian terrorists. The militants had broken into an apartment, dragged a father and two children outside of the building, then shot and killed them. When the violence was over, neighbors rushed into the apartment and found the mother of that family hiding in a closet, holding her baby tightly to her chest. Soon they realized that the terrified mother had held the baby so closely that she had smothered it. Within minutes her entire family had died.

I remember looking down from the TV screen into the face of my brand new son, easily imagining what the mother might have felt looking at her dead baby, and I wept. In fact, I cried off and on for months over this tragedy. I think I grieved with this mother in every way an outsider could – with my emotions, my imagination, my prayers. I'm not sure I could have grieved more if she had been one of my own sisters.

My prayers called out to Jesus to comfort the woman, to heal her mind, to ease her in the way only He could. I wanted to send encouraging messages to this woman: that she forgive herself for the accidental smothering of the baby; that she look to God for hope and for comfort; that she resist harboring hate in her heart for the terrorists, knowing from experience that bitterness could strangle her own life. But I would never see this woman or get to speak to her. I didn't even know her name. So I had to leave all these messages for her with Jesus.

Gradually, as my sorrow lessened, I thought of the woman less often. One day, after nearly two years of praying for this woman from time to time, she again came to my mind. I started to pray for her when something stopped me. Oddly, I felt an overwhelming sense that I didn't need to pray for her any more, that this woman's pain was fading in the same way my own grief for her had dimmed. The idea entered my thoughts that she was healing and finding peace, that all was well.

This sense of knowing about someone else was a strange experience for me. I looked at this strong sense of knowing that the woman was healing alongside the fact that I simply couldn't muster any energy to pray for her in the way I used to, and I concluded that this must be the Holy Spirit's way of letting me know there was no more need for me to pray for her. So I thanked God for helping her and left the episode behind.

Ever since that newscast about the Israeli woman and her family, I had made sure I was never again in the room when the TV news was on. But three years later, in the spring of 1981, I was caught again, nestled on the couch nursing my new baby daughter, when the evening news was switched on. To my astonishment, the news broadcaster was announcing a follow-up story on the Jewish mother who had tragically lost her family three years before. There on my living room television screen was a news reporter actually interviewing the mother. For the first time, I saw her face! She was in her living room in Israel, sitting on a couch next to a new husband and holding their new, nine-month-old baby!

Though the reporter kept pressing the young mother to dwell on the past horror of losing her first family, the woman resisted. Instead, she spoke about how God had comforted her; how she had chosen to let go of the past and move on with her life; how she felt hope and purpose for herself, for her new family and for her country.

I wept for joy, of course! As I listened to her, I could see that all my prayers and hopes for this woman had been answered. And I wept because God had been so kind to me as to make sure that I would see the evening news that night and receive such an unmistakable gift.

I processed this entire spiritual event in my mind and through talking with others to try to understand what had happened. Eventually, my mother loaned me a book entitled *Rees Howells, Intercessor.*[2] This classic biography presented a sequential model of intercessory prayer work that mirrored my own prayer experience:

First, some kind of heart-to-heart identification with the sufferer occurs. Next, a sacrifice or risk is voluntarily offered on behalf of the sufferer. The sacrifice may be as simple as climbing out of bed in the middle of the night to pray or it may be much more extensive. Lastly, according to the book, the intercessor eventually experiences a sense of conclusion that God has heard and is responding. The intercessor may never know the final outcome.

In this early, experiential lesson on the effectiveness of intercessory prayer, I learned an important thing about

God. God can gather up anything we have to offer—including tender tears, post-pregnancy hormones, vivid imagination, sensitivity to suffering, homebound hours or anything else—and use it all to include us in God's life-giving work, even on the other side of the globe.

Wade In the Water

USUALLY I CAN hardly wait to get to the beach along Lake Michigan. It's like holy ground to me. I always breathe more deeply there; feel closer to God there as I take in the beauty. And I love to play in the waves.

But the happily anticipated summer getaway weekend with my spouse had already soured by the time we pulled into the beach parking lot. We'd had another argument. This time it felt like the last straw.

Discouragement and depression were already dogging me. Now I felt utterly hopeless. I could see no way out.

I carried my beach things from the car, dropped them in the sand, and starting wading out into the calm water. The lake stretched out forever, the sky meeting it, blue to blue. I kept walking until I stood neck deep, then stopped. I stood with arms stretched out from my sides to maintain balance as the water moved past me toward shore, when I realized I had no more strength. No more strength to swim out; no strength to walk back; no more strength to go on living. *Should I keep walking out into water over my head until I drown? Could I just sit down right here where I am and simply rest for awhile?* No, you'd drown that way, too, I told myself. I didn't really want to die, I reasoned. I was just too tired to go on with my life the way it was. Too tired to keep trying. Just too tired.

I looked up at the azure sky touching endless, shining water and raised my attention to God. Immediately I felt His presence there with me in and around the water — a kind of unseen weight of being exuding sympathy, understanding, and love. I wept.

After a while, I broke the silence.

"Lord, I know You've been listening to my thoughts," I spoke aloud. "And I'm actually having suicidal thoughts, although I don't really want to die. But I have no more strength to live. I don't know how to go on." More silence. Finally, I cried out, angrily, "Don't You have anything to say to me about all this?"

I waited there in the water for I don't know how long, the frustration seeping out of me. We remained together in the silence, my torso rocking gently with the waves. I felt no sense of condemnation or shame; simply God's loving, immense presence. I stood waiting with expectancy, hoping for anything — a scripture, a phrase, a sign — anything that would give me the strength to live.

Finally, after a long, slow delay, God whispered one word into my mind. One word that was so far removed from my own chaotic thoughts that I knew it couldn't have come from me. God said, "Regeneration."

A huff of incredulous laughter burst from my mouth.

"That's it?" I responded toward the blue sky. "That's all You have to say to me?" I paused.

"Lord, I know You meant this as a word of hope, but I hardly even know what regeneration means." My first thought was of some third grade science lesson about how, if a reptile gets its tail cut off, a new one will grow in its place. Then my mind flitted to thick tomes written by theologians on the subject of regeneration.

But the word and its meaning and what God meant by it for me stirred up my curiosity (which Jesus knew would happen). And the curiosity generated just enough energy in me to turn around and walk back out of the water with newly-kindled hope.

Looking back after more than a decade after this event, I still ponder the meaning of that one word. Dictionary definitions include "the restoration or new growth of that which has been injured or lost" and "to change radically and for the better." Scripture says, "Not by works done in righteousness, which we did ourselves, but according to his mercy [God our Savior] saved us, through the washing of regeneration and renewing of the Holy Spirit" (Titus 3:5, American Standard Version).

All I know is, my return to shore that day marked the beginning of a healing, regenerative process for me. Over time, the Great Physician has removed much of what was emotionally, physically, and spiritually toxic in me. His Spirit continues to replace the empty spaces with new, healthy ways of thinking and being. I am being made new.

"The Christians are distinguished from other men neither by country, nor language, nor the customs which they observe. For they neither inhabit cities of their own, nor employ a peculiar form of speech, nor lead a life which is marked out by any singularity... They dwell in their own countries, but simply as sojourners. As citizens, they share in all things with others, and yet endure all things as if foreigners. Every foreign land is to them as their native country, and every land of their birth as a land of strangers... They are in the flesh, but they do not live after the flesh. They pass their days on earth, but they are citizens of heaven. They obey the prescribed laws, and at the same time surpass the laws by their lives. They love all men, and are persecuted by all... They are poor, yet make many rich... To sum up all in one word – what the soul is in the body, that are Christians in the world."

Letter to Diognetes, c. A.D. 150

Political Jesus

I WATCHED THAT 9/11 terrorist attack of 2001 on the restaurant's television screen during a breakfast meeting in Mid-Michigan. For me, the days following that Tuesday were an amalgamated blur of grief, fear, numbness, and kneeling.

During my morning prayer time on the Friday after, the Spirit brought into my mind the scene of the extraordinary demolition of the Twin Towers in New York City. Into this picture, Jesus suddenly entered, wearing flowing traditional Middle Eastern garb and Converse tennis shoes. He was walking everywhere around Ground Zero, moving this way and that with purposeful strides. No one could see Him. But everywhere He went, everywhere He moved the air, everywhere He breathed, kindness was done. As I meditated upon this image, I understood that my weeping over the past few days had also been His tears of grief over the terrorists' action and the anguish it had caused.

The next day, while I was seated alone on a grassy hill in the warm afternoon sun, the image of Jesus walking among the firefighters and the building wreckage again came to mind. Then a map of Afghanistan and all of the countries of the Middle East superimposed itself over the prior image. A sense of Jesus' great compassion and His loving kindness began to grow huge within me. It filled me, growing so large that the feeling seemed to spill over into the space around me.

I thought, *Wouldn't it be great if all of the Middle Eastern countries, in fact, if every person in the entire world could experience this great loving kindness of Christ?* The desire in me for others to experience Jesus' great love continued to build in me. Its size became gigantic, weighty. I realized that this was a mere taste of God's own desire.

Then other questions formed in my mind:

What would you do for this to happen, Diane? What would you sacrifice? What would you be willing to give for others around the globe to experience the kindness of Christ?

I thought, *I want to give all with abandon, but...I am afraid.*

So in my mind I took each fear, one at a time, and held it up to God. As we looked at them together, I told God that He would have to free me from them; I couldn't do it myself. I believed God would help me overcome them, as necessary.

What can one woman do? I pondered next, aware of my inadequacy. Immediately an image came into my mind of me helping an Iraqi woman purchase Western-style clothing. This didn't seem very politically correct to me, but it seemed that I was helping her feel comfortable in my country. I quickly accepted that this scene would come true one day.

What else can one woman do? I asked.

Use her voice to speak up for the women who cannot use theirs, the still, small Voice answered.

"Please show me when and how," I prayed; then I went home, expectant for direction.

Within days, rumblings among government officials argued that the United States should "strike back" at Iraq, a possible home to the Trade Center terrorists. Immediately I became concerned for the women—both in

Iraq and in the United States — who would suffer even more than they already were if war was declared. When I heard that people from all over the country planned to march for peace in Washington, D.C. at the end of October, I felt that inner nudge to go, though I had never done such a public action in my life. Before I went, the Spirit gave me two simple, focused prayers to carry on my sign in the march:

"God grieves with mothers touched by war" and,

"Pour the kindness of Christ upon Iraq, not bombs."

I drove from Michigan to D.C. with a friend, marched with tens of thousands, and stood with my sign during a four-hour rally of speeches and chants. News cameras from all over the world recorded my sign. One woman offered to hold my sign up for me for 45 minutes while I rested my arms. A Middle Eastern-looking man dressed in traditional clothing, stopped, read my sign, and breathed, "Oh, thank you."

We know by now, of course, that neither the march nor my prayers stopped the war from happening. I consoled myself by believing I had acted faithfully for the concern Jesus had placed inside me.

One summer a few years later, I applied to the World Relief organization in my new home in Nashville to become a volunteer mentor to any Iraqi refugee woman they wanted to assign to me. The interviewing caseworker told me she would call me when she determined the match. I waited four months before I finally got the telephone call. The caseworker said she had found just the right woman and her husband for me to befriend. My heart pounded excitedly at the good news; I felt an immediate flooding of love for this couple I had not yet met.

Soon I was introduced to Hana and her loving husband. They were political refugees offered sanctuary by our country from life-threatening persecution. Hana has learned some English from TV shows. One day she translated the meaning of her name for me, which means "peaceful and happy." This is how I want Hana to be in this country, after all the trauma and loss she has experienced because of war. So I do what I can: drive her to doctor appointments, explain their junk mail, exchange recipes, pray for them. And, yes, because she asked me to, I've even taken her shopping for Western-style clothing. We are friends.

I think Jesus has a way of redeeming everything, of turning bad things inside out for good, of making all things new in His perfect timing. One day I asked Hana what day she and her husband had arrived in the United States.

She looked at me with her wondrous brown eyes and said, "September 11th."

In A Jam
~ a prayer journal entry ~

JESUS, YESTERDAY WAS a beautiful August summer day. Early in the morning, I bought peaches at the Farmers Market to make homemade jam for Christmas presents. I like doing harvest activities like this, Lord. I feel like I'm in Your seasonal rhythm and I somehow feel closer to You and to Your work of sustaining us.

I had already made one successful batch, and was nearly done cutting up the fruit for the second batch, when I realized I wasn't going to have enough peaches. I needed ¾ of a cup more and I was certain the one peach I'd tossed aside in the sink couldn't provide enough. I had set aside that one peach in the first place because most of it was already dark and mushy. Overripe fruit, according to the Sure-Jell product instructions, could mess up the jamming process. So I would have to drive to the store just to get two or three peaches.

Standing there alone in my tiny galley kitchen, it occurred to me to pray about the situation. I wondered out loud to You if this could be a loaves and fishes moment or like the Old Testament woman whose oil never ran out. But my mind immediately censored that thought. It wasn't like I was destitute. *Why don't you ask Me?* I thought I heard You Say. Then I told You I didn't want to test You or anything like that. *Yes, I believe You can do it,* my thoughts continued, *but I don't know if You want to.*

And You asked into my mind, *Do you want Me to?* And I laughed and answered, "Well, sure, it would be so much more convenient for me, but I could go to the store. I don't want to ask this because I'm lazy." I felt an inner nudge to have faith that You wanted to do this for me. I guess I believed the nudge because the next thing I said out loud, with a nervous giggle, was, "How do I do this with You? Am I supposed to cut up the fruit and then turn my head away or something, while You double it? Am I supposed to watch? Will the cut-up fruit piled on the cutting board just puff up?"

But I felt game for the adventure and started peeling the mushy peach. I deftly cut off all the overripe part of the fruit, knowing by experience there wasn't enough left to fill up the measuring cup. As I had done with all the other peaches, I pressed the knife in all the way to the pit, to divide the pulp and pull it off in chunks that I would chop into smaller pieces. My mind acknowledged in passing that my knife went much deeper into peach flesh than I expected. I thought, "This pit must be unusually small."

Then I chopped up the chunks and paused a moment to look at the little pile on the cutting board. I still wondered if it would be enough. I started scooping the pulp up by hand and dropping it into the glass measuring cup. Then I tipped my head sideways to see if the contents leveled out to the one cup line, and they did. Exactly.

The truth took a moment to sink in. When my brain finally comprehended what my eyes were seeing, I was undone. I suddenly doubled over, feeling as if a needle had pierced the center of my body. I backed out of the kitchen and began weeping. Weeping for the fact that You had done this for me. A small thing simply for my convenience. A huge thing because You showed me how much You love me, as I am, in the middle of simple chores. And I am still moved to the core of my soul, my mind is blown away (what are the adequate words for this?) that You are God and that You want to serve me. Together these two facts are astonishing.

I can only conclude that You are the Servant-King. You do not abuse Your power. Your Love delicately enters our lives in a way that won't crush us, we who are "just dust," after all. Yet apparently I'm cherished dust. Who can understand it? My throat swells at such tenderness and the wonder of it.

I will say this, and You are welcome to remind me of it any time I might begin to act otherwise:

I want nothing or no one to interfere with our relationship. Forever.

The Perfect Rescue

SHE SAID, "WE'RE gonna make it happen!" and they did. My two kayaking buddies arranged for us to take an early April paddle down the Chippewa River, squeezing the ride into a brief time slot in my busy schedule while visiting back home in Michigan. Off and on for years Kathy and Deb and I had enjoyed leisurely floating down the "Chip" in our kayaks—not the kind of kayak you see on TV where people are secured into tight kayak aprons and do 360° flips in white water. No, our recreational kayaks look more like little canoes, offering wide open access for one person to sit and move around as they paddle flat water.

The three of us had become addicted to what I call "river time," when our minds slow down to the lazy pace of the water. Stress just drains away as we gaze at the slowly passing scenery. We usually float down the river during warm summer months. That's when the river can get so shallow that we have to step out, getting our ankles wet dragging our vessels along the scratchy river bottom into deeper water. Sometimes we chat, catching up on family news. Sometimes we paddle silently, leaving sunning turtle families undisturbed on their logs. When a great heron rises up from around a river bend, we point and smile at each other, and consider our trip complete.

But today, after a snowy, record-breaking winter, the riverbed was flooded with deep, rapid, icy currents—

a contrast to the warm, spring air that felt like summer. Celebrating old times before I headed back to Tennessee, we tossed our life preserver cushions into our individual kayaks, slipped the hulls into the high water, and began rhythmically dipping our oars with the confidence of seasoned paddlers.

Not until we rounded a curve about halfway along our route did our casual conversation stop mid-sentence. Just ahead a huge, newly fallen tree lay across the river, and the swollen current sped us toward it. With my kayak out in front and only seconds to change my course, I quickly scanned the trunk's length, seeking a spot that would let me go around the tree rather than crash into it. From behind, Kathy shouted: "I think over by the left!" I aimed my kayak toward what looked like an opening—a deceptively inviting arched branch that might let me slip around the trunk. The powerful current immediately rushed my kayak forward toward the hole.

Not until I was right up on it could I see that the overhead arch was attached like a sideways "V" to a nearly- submerged length of horizontal tree limb. Too late to skirt the wood, my kayak became instantly trapped sideways alongside the log, pressed by thousands of gallons of icy river water pouring against its side. Within two seconds the current forced the right side down and began flooding the vessel, quickly flipping the kayak and tossing me out into the shock of ice water completely over my head. My feet couldn't find bottom to push up from, so I quickly pressed my open arms down hard, forcing my head to the surface.

Where's the life preserver when you need it? I thought, as I resurfaced, gasping for breath. That was the moment I realized my chest muscles couldn't expand. They were already contracted from the snow-fed water.

I may only have one more breath, my mind rationalized, and immediately my arms flailed into an adrenaline-charged crawl toward shore. *Would my breath last until I got there? How long before hypothermia turned blood into slush?*

Keep kicking, I willed my freezing legs. Even though the shore was now only two or three body lengths away, I couldn't cross the gap. The powerful current swept me parallel with the edge.

Seeing my swim strokes, Kathy assumed I was fine and zoomed by me to retrieve my upside down kayak, now floating downriver. Deb paddled up behind me, asking, "Do you need help?"

"Yes!" I answered with as little breath as possible. The length of her kayak curved around in front of me, blocking my course. With one arm, Deb stretched out her oar, which I grabbed. Then she pulled my body to shore, keeping her kayak steady with her other hand by grasping nearby foliage. My stiff legs scrambled up onto the sand and I sat down, shaky but alive! Soon the sun warmed my muscles, allowing air to fill my lungs.

"Are you okay?" Deb asked from her kayak, her eyes searching my face.

"Yes," I grinned, "since I lived!" Relieved, she laughed and turned to paddle downstream toward Kathy, who had retrieved my kayak and oar, the floating life preserver, and one water shoe.

The whole incident probably lasted less than three minutes. At the time it happened, I didn't pray or feel fear or see "life-passing-before-my-eyes"—I could only focus on surviving. Now that I had a moment to catch my breath, I shuddered. The accident could have ended in disaster. Instead, my friends had just executed a perfect rescue mission.

And didn't they do the very same thing for me a few years ago when my marriage crumbled? I reflected, as I stood up and started walking along the shore to join them. *And during the cancer event a couple years later?* My spill into the river was a perfect metaphor, I decided, for how these women and many other church members had helped me during other near-disasters. Jesus had sent people who came alongside me, helped me pick up the pieces, and set me back on my feet.

Soon my friends and I were on our way again, my kayak upright and floating, my wet clothes beginning to dry in the warm spring air, all of us laughing and joking about our unexpected adventure. I felt braver and freer, somehow, as we continued on toward our destination.

What Really Matters?

I WAS WORRIED that the money would come between us. That's why I was sitting in the darkness of my living room late one Saturday night in the early 1980s — to pray for unity.

My little church — a remnant of a university campus ministry — had just sold its building in preparation for merging with a larger church. Now we had to decide what to do with the money from the sale. The amount totaled more than any one of us was ever likely to spend all at once in their lifetime.

But sometimes money can get between the most loving people, and division was the last thing I wanted to happen. So I for one urged our little band of six families to try to discern as a group how God wanted us to spend the money. We decided to use the prayer and fasting practices we had recently studied in Richard Foster's book *Celebration of Discipline*.[3] Most agreed to fast from Saturday until after church Sunday morning. We would use the hunger pangs as reminders to pray for unity and for guidance about the money.

Now I sat on the edge of my couch, the only light coming from the porch light. It sent yellowish rays through the window, over my shoulder and across the dim room toward the old upright piano.

With my eyes open and facing the piano, I began praying, when suddenly I no longer saw the piano, but a scene of two huge mountains. I was on top of one of the mountains. From my vantage point I could see the other mountain far in the distance, from its top all the way down into the valley below.

On top of that distant mountain were two thrones. I could see The Father's seated frame from the waist down, the folds of His robe draped downward. From the waist up, God was hidden in light and clouds.

At the bottom of God's mountain stood a man who was all light and very tall—almost as tall as the mountain itself. I knew this was Christ ascending to His throne next to the Father. Jesus was full of light and glory as He walked slowly and stately up that mountain. Behind Him flowed a long, wide veil like a bridal train that began at the back of His head and flowed down behind Him, trailing for miles and miles between the two mountains like a beautiful river. The veil was completely composed of sparkling dots of light—millions and millions of tiny sparkles shimmering with the intensity of diamond prisms or light-reflecting sequins.

Swiftly my view changed as I swooped down my mountain toward the sparkling veil. As I got closer, my eyes seemed to be looking through telescopic lenses. The lenses focused for a close-up look at the shimmering veil until I could see that every point of dazzling sparkle was a person! I saw millions and millions of shining faces of the Holy Ones slowly, happily ascending up the mountain with Jesus to be presented to His Father.

If I moved my eyes away from these lenses, the faces dissolved back into the brilliant dazzle of the river-like veil. I looked back through the lenses and next my vision zoomed in on a section of the last third of the veil. I saw individual people dressed in European Renaissance clothing of the 1600s. Behind them followed people clothed as Pilgrims of the 1700s; then clothing of the United States "Wild West" era; then clothing of 1920s styles right up to people dressed as my own contemporaries. I realized the veil was a living time line of the church. Millions of people were laughing and joyous and back-slapping; they knew where they were going and that they would arrive there soon.

Suddenly — in the midst of that crowd — I saw myself! There I was in my own era of history, surrounded by people of my culture that I knew while I was alive on Earth. My arms were around the shoulders of two people walking on either side of me. We were walking toward Jesus, and I am laughing and shouting joyfully with everyone else. I saw myself smiling, and then turning my head I said to those behind me, "We're here! We're here! We made it!" I felt my own excitement and joy that my loved ones and I were there, moving in the winding bridal train, ready to be proudly presented by Jesus to the Father.

As I watched myself in the crowd, my view gradually became unfocused. The image of me and the others slowly blended back into the mass of dazzling lights which now made up the gorgeous bridal veil. As I watched intently, the scene faded until I found myself staring across at the old, brown piano in my living room.

From that night to this present time, I know to the core of my being that nothing — nothing — is more important than being in that crowd on the day when Jesus presents His Holy Ones.

The vision also confirmed my mission while on Earth: to cheer others on toward God. Even now, decades later, I try to prioritize most everything I do under the general heading of encouragement. I feel most fulfilled when I am carrying out this role.

And what happened to the little band of church friends who fasted and prayed about how to spend the money from the sale of the building? First of all, we rookie fasters learned to never break a fast with pizza-all-meat-extra-cheese.

We also planned a meeting in the backyard of one of the families. Each came prayerfully prepared with a favorite charity in mind plus an amount they wanted to donate to that charity. Our treasurer wrote down each organization and suggested amount as each person in the circle presented their hope. The wide diversity of charities ranged from a ranch for boys to a grace-oriented religious magazine to the new church we were merging with and more.

We waited while the treasurer added up the amounts, then he announced a surprising outcome. The total amount of our wishes came to exactly half the amount of the sale. When we realized that each of us could *double* the amount we wanted to give, there was stunned silence. Suddenly, spontaneously, the entire group simultaneously jumped up from our chairs and began laughing and clapping for joy!

That unity of celebrating hearts was a tiny taste of our future walk in the veil.

Made-Up
True
Stories

The Parable of the Wild Dog

"And if your right hand causes you to sin, cut it off and throw it away; it is better for you to lose one of your members than for your whole body to go into hell." ~ Matthew 5:30, NRSV

ONCE UPON A time there was a man who had inherited a wild dog. The dog lived on property that the man's father had owned. Most people stayed away from wild dogs like this one; they were unreliable as pets, often biting the hands that fed them.

This wild dog was no different. But as a child, the man had spied on his father one day, following him out to the back forty acres. To his surprise the boy's dad set out a piece of meat for the wild dog, then stood a short distance away. The snarling dog came near, voraciously ate the meat, then looked up at the man. The man threw a stick from his hand, and the dog ran to fetch it, galloping back to drop it a few feet away from the man for more play.

The boy had seen this, and now that he was a man he had imitated his father's behavior. His relationship with the wild dog was one of the most exciting things in his life. The adrenaline rush the man experienced every time the dog came near was thrilling, addictive. Would the dog bite him? Play with him? Eat the meat? Reject him? Want more? These variables made life interesting for the man. He was a solid, respectable family man. But sometimes he craved the spice of more daring adventures than his everyday life usually offered. And so visiting the wild dog from time to time went on for years.

But one day everything changed. The wild dog followed the man home and hung around the family yard. Jealous for more food and attention from the man, the wild dog would lunge viciously at the man's beloved children or his wife. The first time the wild dog actually bit one of his children, the man caught the dog and chained him up.

But this was a wild dog, strong and untamed and used to surviving on his own terms. He broke the man's chain time and again, attacking the man and his family members at will. The children, hurt and confused that their loving father would allow such a beast to live and endanger them all, gradually distanced themselves from their father. The man, who had always apologized for the wild dog's behavior, couldn't bring himself to get rid of the dog.

"What would I do for excitement?" he thought. "I feel so alive when the wild dog is around. He seems like a part of me after all these years. And wouldn't I be dishonoring my own father if I let go of this portion of my inheritance?"

After making that choice, the man grew old, his scars multiplied, his life felt more and more isolated. Eventually, the man died.

One day, a few years later, a young man climbed a hill on the property he had inherited from his father. The land was beautiful—green and rich and fruitful. But off in the distance something caught his eye—it was the wild dog, a portion of his earthly inheritance.

"What shall I do about the wild dog?" the young man asked himself, as he began moving through the tall grass to get a better look.

He Spoke My Name
Mary Magdalene Remembers

Dramatic reading based upon Matthew 27:55-56, 28:1-11;
Luke 8:1-3, 23:27-31, 49, 55-56; 24:1-11; John 20:1-18

I hated those voices!

For years those voices echoed in my head, tormenting me. They laughed at my body. They made fun of my face, my nose… my eyes.

Sometimes they attacked my ability to think. No matter what choice I'd make, they would scream: "Fool!" "Idiot!" "Worthless woman!"

The voices mocked me relentlessly day and night. They shattered my sanity. Demolished my confidence. Convinced me—and everyone else in town—that I was the Shame of Magdala.

Then Jesus spoke to me.

Somehow on that day the jostling crowd pushed me right into a space where the new, young rabbi was standing. His kind eyes looked straight into mine and He asked,

"What is your name?"

But the voices answered Him with seven different names that were not mine at all!

Jesus ignored their answers. His voice reached into

the center of my mind and, in spite of the din, I could again hear Him ask: "What is your name?" I felt so grateful that this kind man would look for me—the true me—in the middle of all those invasive voices.

Then Jesus firmly told those voices to "Get out!" In an instant they were gone!

Who would have thought that the course of my life would be entirely altered through such simple words spoken by this homespun rabbi?

After that, I followed Him everywhere. I had to hear what else He had to say. His teachings were good and sane and soothing to my tired mind and spirit. Slowly, I gained the courage to trust myself again. I actually started making new friends with some of the other women who followed Him. We all helped the Teacher with His ministry. All of us loved Him!

Yes, I was there when those soldiers killed Jesus.

I was certain I'd never hear Him say my name again.

But I did.

That morning after the Sabbath when I stood outside His empty tomb and I was certain those soldiers had stolen His body and I was crying so hard and someone behind me asked why I was crying and I babbled something back at them but then—the Voice spoke my name in that way that nobody else says it:

"Mary."

I turned around and I looked at Him. And suddenly astonishment and joy and relief and questions and deep, deep love knotted so tightly in my throat that only one word could escape in response:

"Teacher!"

Communion
Meditations

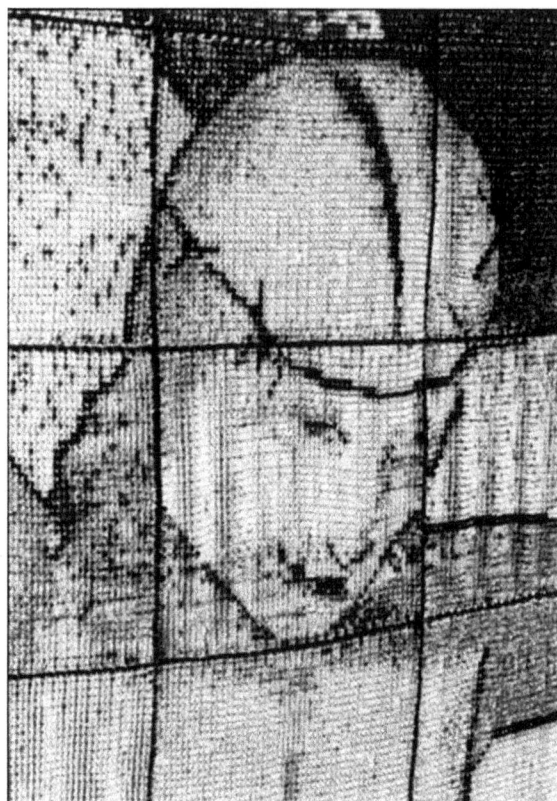

Note to Readers

During a bout of illness one summer, I was invited by Jesus to make a change in my diet by meeting Him each day through the taking of communion. The Lord's Supper has always been very meaningful to me, so I eagerly answered "Yes!" and quickly stocked up on grape juice and flat bread.

Quietly meeting Jesus nearly daily through the tangible elements of bread and juice or wine is never dull or boring. Sometimes these encounters are startlingly fresh; sometimes they feel familiar. But no two moments are alike when I'm with this creative God who delights in making all things new.

The collective result of meeting Jesus through daily communion is that my mind and heart and spirit have become more deeply entwined with Him. I feel more grounded, more deeply rooted. Some of the following reflections are a sample of my earlier internal responses to joining Jesus daily in this sacred rite of grace.

We Are Starving for God

We are starving for God.
We don't know it, but we are.
Like anorexic thinking, we believe we're full—maybe too much so.
Or we eat and eat and eat,
        but still know hunger; still feel empty.

When we channel surf, we are starving for God.
When we fill every silence with song, sound, and talk, we starve for God.
When we drug 'til numb, we starve for God.
Seek serial sex with multiple partners, we starve for God.
When hobbies turn compulsive and drive away the joy,
        we starve for God.
When we strain with ambition to promote only ourselves,
        we starve for God.

When we people-please,
Build stashes of treasures,
Stockpile defenses,
Control everything we can because we can,
we
are
starving
for
God.
We just don't know it.

But now we do.

So here is our personal invitation—an antidote from heaven—
from the Personal God who whispers to each of us:
"Eat! Please eat!
This is My Body.
Let the cells of this bread be absorbed inside you and take Me
with it.
Let Me nourish you.
Let Me fill you up with what truly satiates your deep need
        for friendship with the One who loves you most.
I know what you need and I will fill the void.

"Drink! Drink!
Let this wine that is My Blood mingle with yours to
        cleanse you,
        feed you,
        make you new.

"Eat of Me until your hunger stops.
Drink of Me until your thirst is gone.
Only then will you be:
        satisfied,
        purified,
        consecrated,
        strengthened to
walk out these doors and back into the world."

Hallelujah!

Waiting

As I sat with communion bread gripped in my hand, my mind wandered off for I don't know how long. When suddenly I remembered the bread held tightly, and that You were still there, waiting patiently for my mind's return.

Briefly I felt shy, self-disparaging, embarrassed that I'd kept You — of all beings — waiting for so long.

But You smiled, patient as usual, ready to be present in the Eucharistic sacrament.

At that moment I realized this is Your stance:
You wait and wait and wait for us to give You
a glance,
a moment,
a small segment of our time.

You wait and wait and wait to be a
Friend to us; a Lifeguard;
Physician to our woundedness;
Nanny to our inner child;
Comedian to our low spirits;
Bridegroom to our tender hearts;
Coworker in life's purposes;
Wise One to our questionings;
Hero to our need to worship
Someone greater than ourselves.

You wait and wait and wait for us to be with You.

A Sales Pitch for Communion

Ladies and Gentlemen—
    Step right up to the table of our Lord, the One and
Only True God!
    If you believe even a little itty bit that Jesus is the
Son of God, you will benefit from the amazing nutrition of
what appears to be flimsy wafer and splash of grape juice
because,
once ingested,
these humble elements may infuse the believing eater with
        near-magical powers!

For some, fear vanishes and courage pours into their veins.
Others taste their Savior and know for sure that abandonment
is never in His game plan for them.
Scales drop from some eyes and people suddenly see Jesus
in desperate disguises
which ignites a passion to run and offer:
        cups of fresh water,
        comforting kindnesses,
        shelter from the darkness of the soul.

Come one! Come all!
Wondrous gifts await you!
Promised through this delicate feast—
        pre-paid indelicately
        by the Lord of Abundant Grace.

Will you come?

A Prayer for Realigned Appetites
(Can be used as responsive reading)

When Illusion drapes its veil across my sight,
> Wipe my eyes clear, O God, that I may see the Truth.

When I begin to fill my hollow sorrow with things other
than You,
> Please stop me cold.

For bitter turns the taste of this world's cake.
> Yet appetite for Bread of Life is weak.

The twisted rope of my quite crooked ways chokes off the
life that you have hoped for me.
> Only Your Power unravels tangled knots like mine.

Make my path straight to You,
> My will just like Your own.

Illuminate my eyes with Your pure Love,
> And make my self a place You can call home.

Dancing in Heaven

In my mind I'm already dancing
In ways my flesh cannot possibly perform.
But there will be a day
When my spirit will reflect
The rainbow of Your Light
And I shall dance to You freely
In Spirit-powered praise
All of the days forevermore.

Acknowledgements

I thank God for the opportunity to share these stories, and for the people He sent to help me with this project.

With a grateful heart, I say "thanks" for the weekly positive support and friendly critiques from *The Franklin FaithWriters*, which encouraged me to go public with the stories in this book.

Several individuals from this group added invaluable practical help in addition to cheering me on: Author and graphic designer Christina Nelson created the amazing cover and did the layout while offering professional advice and encouragement; author Julie Tomsett gave hours of business acumen and practical discernment; writer and editor Tyra Brumfield applied her professional expertise to the entire content and was still willing to add her encouraging endorsement; and author Irmgard Williams took time from her busy schedule to add a complimentary recommendation, too. I also want to thank Joel and Carol Tomlin, the owners of *Landmark Booksellers* in Franklin, TN, who provide hospitable gathering spaces for *The Franklin FaithWriters* and many other authors.

My appreciation also extends to professional writer, editor, and long-time friend Noreen Bryant, who edited the copy, offered key suggestions, and wrote a generous-hearted endorsement. And thanks to my sister Judy L. Ide, who has heard most of these stories before, yet was willing to read the written versions, to offer her wise insight, and to believe in the purpose of this book.

I also feel gratitude to *Yatsar*, long-time spiritual friend and professional artist, who knew I was writing a book before I even told her.

Thanks to John and Myra Ishee of J M Press, Inc. for their friendly, timely, first-class service.

And I feel grateful to God for the many people who have prayed for me and for this book. This includes my family, long-time friends and new ones, particularly my *unveil* prayer group at The Anchor Fellowship in Nashville, and my spiritual directors peer supervision group.

Endnotes

[1] Phillips, J.B. <u>Your God Is Too Small</u>. Macmillan Publishing Company, 1961.
[2] Grubb, Norman. <u>Rees Howells, Intercessor</u>. CLC Publications, 1959.
[3] Foster, Richard. <u>Celebration of Discipline</u>. HarperCollins, 1983.

www.ingramcontent.com/pod-product-compliance
Lightning Source LLC
Chambersburg PA
CBHW071843020426
42331CB00007B/1839